Vietnam

by Joyce Markovics

Consultant: Marjorie Faulstich Orellana, PhD
Professor of Urban Schooling
University of California, Los Angeles

New York, New York

Credits

TOC, © tristan tan/Shutterstock; 4, © Galyna Andrushko/Shutterstock; 5L, © Frank Fischbach/Shutterstock; 5R, © R.M. Nunes/Shutterstock; 7, © RobertDodge/iStock; 8–9, © gnomeandi/Shutterstock; 9, © Hang Dinh/Shutterstock; 10, © Colette3/Shutterstock; 11T, © Eugene_Sim/iStock; 11B, © kajornyot/Shutterstock; 12–13, © beboy/Shutterstock; 13, © Lester Balajadia/Shutterstock; 14, © Vietnam Photography/Shutterstock; 15T, © PrasitRodphan/Shutterstock; 15B, © Hemis/Alamy; 16–17, © vinhdav/Shutterstock; 17T, ©Onfokus/iStock; 18, © Photographic Art Viet Nam/Shutterstock; 19, © AleksandarTodorovic/Dreamstime; 20, © kelvin tran/Shutterstock; 21, © naluwan/Shutterstock; 22, © Saigon Photography/Shutterstock; 23, © Duc Den Thui/Shutterstock; 24, © jethuynh/Shutterstock; 25, © Jimmy Tran/Shutterstock; 26, © 123stocks/iStock; 27T, © HongVo/Shutterstock; 27B, © Moon Nguyen/Shutterstock; 28, © Photoshot/Newscom; 29, © Pal2iyawit/Shutterstock; 30 (T to B), © fourleaflover/Shutterstock, © oleg_Mit/Shutterstock, © Scruggelgreen/Shutterstock, and © MaksNarodenko/Shutterstock; 31 (T to B), © vinhdav/Shutterstock, © beboy/Shutterstock, © Galyna Andrushko/Shutterstock, and © RichardWhitcombe/Shutterstock; 32, © noppharat/Shutterstock.

Publisher: Kenn Goin
Senior Editor: Joyce Tavolacci
Creative Director: Spencer Brinker
Design: Debrah Kaiser
Photo Researcher: Olympia Shannon

Special Thanks to Robert Faulstich for his help reviewing this book.

Library of Congress Cataloging-in-Publication Data

Markovics, Joyce L., author.
  Vietnam / by Joyce Markovics.
      pages cm. — (Countries we come from)
  Includes bibliographical references and index.
  Audience: Age 4–8.
  ISBN 978-1-62724-860-0 (library binding) — ISBN 1-62724-860-9 (library binding)
  1. Vietnam—Juvenile literature. I. Title.
  DS556.3.M37 2016
  959.7—dc23
                                       2015004745

For more information, write to Bearport Publishing Company, Inc., 45 West 21st Street, Suite 3B, New York, New York 10010. Printed in the United States of America.

10 9 8 7 6 5 4 3 2 1

Contents

Tropical

Beautiful

Friendly

Vietnam is in Southeast Asia.

More than 93 million people live there.

Vietnam

Arctic Ocean

NORTH
AMERICA

EUROPE

ASIA

Atlantic
Ocean

AFRICA

Pacific
Ocean

Pacific
Ocean

SOUTH
AMERICA

Indian
Ocean

N

W   E

AUSTRALIA

S

Southern Ocean

ANTARCTICA

Vietnam is a long,
S-shaped country.

What types of land are in Vietnam?

Tall mountains stretch across the north.

Flat land covers the south.

Thick jungles cover many of the mountains.

Sandy beaches run along the coast.

Many rare animals live in Vietnam.
Tigers roam the jungles.

Giant catfish swim in the rivers.

Colorful birds fly in the sky.

More than 800 kinds of birds live in Vietnam.

a farmer growing rice

The weather is **tropical**.
It's warm and wet.
It's good for farming.
Rice is Vietnam's main **crop**.

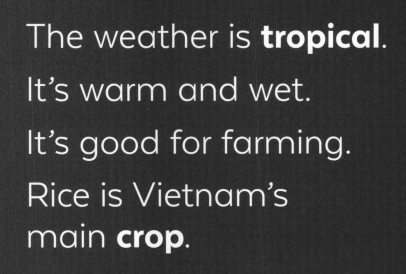

Sometimes, huge storms called **typhoons** hit Vietnam. They bring strong winds and rain.

There are large cities in Vietnam.

Ho Chi Minh (HOH CHEE MIN)
City is the biggest.

The city has hotels and museums.

It also has busy outdoor markets.

Vietnam's biggest sports arena is in Ho Chi Minh City.

flower market

15

Vietnam's **capital** is Hanoi.

The city has many tall buildings.

Many people get around on bikes and motorbikes.

Hanoi is more than 1,000 years old.

PHƯỜNG RỐI NƯỚC LÀNG YÊN
THẠCH XÁ - THẠCH THẤT - HÀ NỘI

In Hanoi, there is a special theater.

It's called the Water Puppet Theater.

The stage is a huge pool of water.

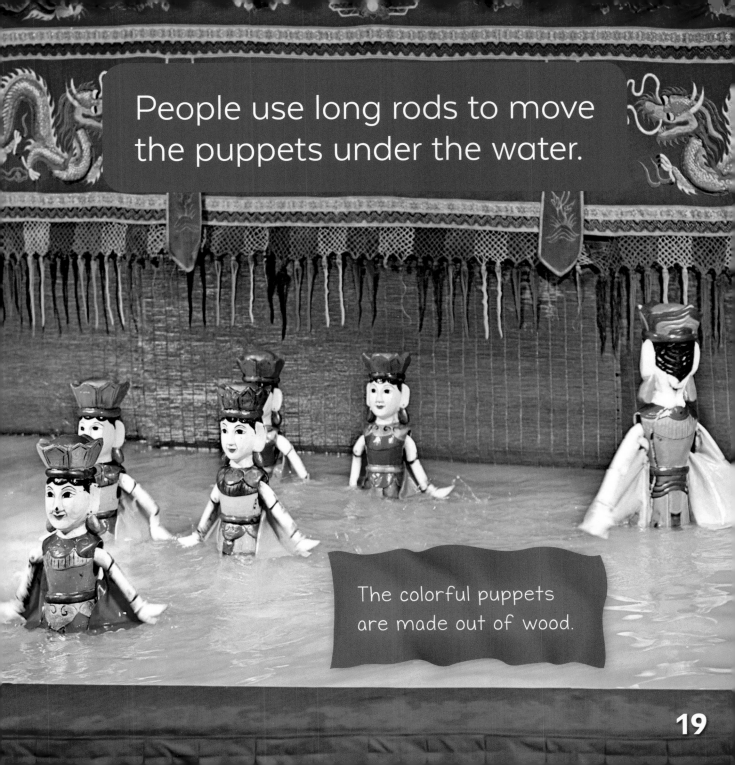

People use long rods to move the puppets under the water.

The colorful puppets are made out of wood.

Most people speak Vietnamese.
This is how you say *hello*:

Xin chào (SIN CHOW)

This is how you say *good-bye*:

Tạm biệt (TOM BEE-et)

The most common last name in Vietnam is Nguyễn (NOO-yen).

The biggest festival in the country is Tết.

Tết is the Vietnamese New Year.

People bang drums and march in parades.

Children get red envelopes filled with money.

People also eat sticky rice cakes for Tết.

sticky rice cake

23

Many women wear áo dàis (AW dahys).

They are long dresses with slits.

Áo dàis come in many bright colors.

Áo dài are worn over pants.

Foods in Vietnam are colorful and tasty.

Most dishes include fresh herbs and fish sauce.

Soups called phở (FUH) are very popular.

They are often made with meat and noodles.

Chè is a sweet dessert. It can be made with beans, fruit, or coconut.

Takraw is a popular sport in Vietnam.

It's like volleyball.

However, you play it with your feet!

Each year, Vietnam holds a Takraw championship.

Fast Facts

Capital city: Hanoi

Population of Vietnam:
More than 93 million

Main language:
Vietnamese

Money: Dong

Major religions: Buddhism,
Confucianism, Taoism, and
Christianity

Neighboring countries:
China, Cambodia, and Laos

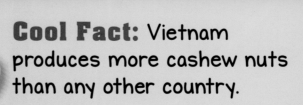

Cool Fact: Vietnam
produces more cashew nuts
than any other country.

capital (KAP-uh-tuhl) a city where a country's government is based

crop (KROP) plants that are grown in large amounts, usually for food

tropical (TROP-i-kuhl) having to do with the warm areas of Earth near the equator

typhoons (tye-FOONZ) hurricanes that occur in the Pacific Ocean near Asia

31

Index

Read More

Kalman, Bobbie. *Vietnam the Land (Lands, Peoples, and Cultures).* New York: Crabtree (2002).

Willis, Terri. *Vietnam (Enchantment of the World).* New York: Scholastic (2013).

Learn More Online

To learn more about Vietnam, visit
www.bearportpublishing.com/CountriesWeComeFrom

About the Author

Joyce Markovics lives far from Vietnam in
Tarrytown, New York.